My Best Bear Hug

Donna Alvermann
Connie A. Bridge
Barbara A. Schmidt
Lyndon W. Searfoss
Peter Winograd
Scott G. Paris

The bear on the cover was drawn by first-grader Matthew Kitchen from Thorpe Elementary School in Sterling Heights, MI.

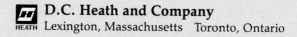

D.C. Heath and Company
Lexington, Massachusetts   Toronto, Ontario

Acknowledgments

Grateful acknowledgment is made for permission to reprint the following copyrighted material.

Anderson, Marjorie Allen. "**A New Friend**" is reprinted by permission of *Highlights for Children,* copyright 1950.

Begay, Sandra. "**Why Bears Have Short Tails**," from *And It Is Still That Way,* copyright © 1976 by Byrd Baylor. Reprinted by permission of Scribner's Book Company.

Douglass, Barbara. "**Good As New**" is adapted by permission of Lothrop, Lee & Shepard Books (a division of William Morrow & Company). Copyright © 1982 by Barbara Douglass.

Gackenbach, Dick. "**Wishes for Hattie**," from *Hattie Rabbit,* copyright © 1976 by Dick Gackenbach, is reprinted by permission of Harper & Row, Publishers, Inc.

Ginsburg, Mirra. **Mushroom in the Rain** is reprinted by permission of Macmillan Publishing Company, copyright © 1974.

Holl, Adelaide. **The Rain Puddle** is reprinted by permission of Lothrop, Lee & Shepard Books (a division of William Morrow & Company). Copyright © 1965.

Johnston, Tony. "**The Stranger**," from *Odd Jobs and Friends,* is reprinted by permission of G.P. Putnam's Sons, copyright © 1982.

Lobel, Arnold. "**The Surprise**," from *Frog and Toad All Year,* copyright © 1976 by Arnold Lobel, is reprinted by permission of Harper & Row, Publishers, Inc.

Orleans, Ilo. "**Paints**" is reprinted by permission of Mrs. Orleans.

Santos, S. Elsie. "**The Frog in the Bog**" is reprinted by permission of Shawme Enterprises from *Stories for Young Grandchildren,* by Grandma Elsie. Copyright © 1986. All rights reserved.

Udry, Janice May. "**What Mary Jo Shared**" is reprinted by permission of Albert Whitman & Company. Copyright © 1966.

Cover   **Design:** Ken Silvia Design Group.   **Illustration:** Matthew Kitchen.

Grateful acknowledgment is made for contributions from the following teachers and their students:
Pamela Rosta, Thorpe Elementary School, Sterling Heights, MI.
Eleanor Smith, Bessemer Primary School, Greensboro, NC.

Cluster Openers   **Design:** Studio Goodwin-Sturges.   **Illustration:** Ashley Wolff.   **Calligraphy:** Colleen.

Editorial   Book Editors: Laura A. Tills, Michael P. Gibbons.   **Senior Editor:** Susan D. Paro.   **Editorial Services:** Marianna Frew Palmer, K. Kirschbaum Harvie.   **Permissions Editor:** Dorothy B. McLeod.
Design   Series: Leslie Dews.   Book: Laura E. Fredericks, Meral Dabcovich, Judy Sue Goodwin-Sturges.
Production   Mary Hunter.

Illustration   **8–15:** James Marshall. **17–19:** Laura E. Fredericks. **20:** Lois Ehlert. **24–32:** Krystyna Turska. **34–37:** Gavin Bishop. **38–42:** Dick Gackenbach, copyright © 1976, from *Hattie Rabbit,* with permission. **46–51:** Diane Stanley. **53–55:** Mary Maclaren. **57–64:** Kate Duke. **68–76:** Bernard Wiseman. **80–88:** Tomie de Paola, copyright © 1982, from *Odd Jobs and Friends,* with permission. **92–100:** Arnold Lobel, copyright © 1976, from *Frog And Toad All Year,* with permission. **102–109:** Hans Wilhelm. **110–114:** Dorothea Sierra. **118–129:** Brian Cody. **131–133:** Marc Brown. **134–140:** Phillipe Dupasquier. **144–154:** José Aruego and Ariane Dewey, copyright © 1965, from *Mushroom in the Rain,* with permission. **156–157:** David McPhail. **158–170:** Ronald Himler. **174–178:** Ashley Wolff. **180–181:** Jane Dyer. **182–186:** Holly Berry. **188–203:** Patience Brewster, copyright © 1982, from *Good as New,* with permission. 204–223: Bob Shein.

Photography   **17–20:** Doug Mindell © D.C. Heath. **53:** *l,* Breck P. Kent (Animals Animals); *tr,* © Doug Wechsler; *br,* Oxford Scientific Films (Animals Animals). **54:** *tl,* William E. Ferguson; *tr,* Zig Leszczynski (Animals Animals); *b,* Hans Reinhard (Bruce Coleman, Inc.). **55:** *l,* © Dwight R. Kuhn; *tr,* Donald Specker (Animals Animals); *br,* Breck P. Kent (Animals Animals). **78–79,110–114:** Ken O'Donoghue © D.C. Heath. **174:** © Tom & Pat Leeson. **175:** *tl, bl,* Alan D. Carey; *r,* S.J. Kramer (Peter Arnold). **176:** *c,* Breck P. Kent (Animals Animals); *b,* Steven C. Kaufman (Peter Arnold). **177:** *l,* Mark Chappell (Animals Animals); *r,* Alan D. Carey. **178:** *c,* Wayne Lankinen (DRK Photo); *b,* Michael Gadomski (Earth Scenes/Animals Animals).
Photo Coordinator: Connie Komack.   Photo Research: Martha Friedman.   Photo Styling: Elizabeth Willis.

Published simultaneously in Canada

Printed in the United States of America

International Standard Book Number: 0-669-30042-X

2 3 4 5 6 7 8 9 0 – RRD – 96 95 94 93

Table of Contents

Home Sweet Home

New Friends and Old

2

Wind and Rain

Toys, Toys, Toys

Sharing

Bear Tales

What goes up in the air white and comes down yellow and white? *(an egg)*

What is a cat's favorite color? *(purr-ple)*

Mixing Colors

The Picture
by James Marshall

One day a rabbit came to the beach.

"Wow," he said. "I must paint
a picture of this!"

So he sat down. Soon he had
painted the sky and water.

"This is a lot of fun," he said.
"I really like my picture."

Just then a dog walked by.

"Oh no," said the dog. "That's not right. The sky is too blue. Put in more white."

"No, thank you," said the rabbit. "I like it my way."

"Very well," said the dog. "It's **your** picture." And she went away.

The rabbit went on painting. Soon
a bird came by.

"No, no, no," said the bird. "The
sun is too red. Put in some more yellow.
That will make it orange."

"No, thank you," said the rabbit.
"I like it my way."

"Well, it's **your** picture," said the
bird. And she went away.

The rabbit went on painting. Soon a toad came by.

"Oh my," said the toad. "That water isn't right. It's too green. Put in more blue."

"No, thank you," said the rabbit. "I like it my way."

"Very well," said the toad. "It's **your** picture." And away he went.

"Everyone has something to say,"
said the rabbit.

He went on painting. Just then
a family of bugs came by.

"**Now** what?" said the rabbit.

"Wow!" said the father bug.
"Will you look at that!"

"What a pretty red!" said the mother bug.

"What great greens and blues!" said the bug kids.

"Do you really think so?" said the rabbit.

"Oh yes!" said the bug family.

"Yes?" said the rabbit. "Well then, it's **your** picture."

"May we really have it?" said the
father bug.

"We will put it in our house," said
the mother bug.

"Wow!" said the bug kids.

Then the bug family picked up the
picture to carry it home.

"I wonder how they will get it
in their house," thought the rabbit.

Think About It

1. What did the animals want the rabbit to do with his picture?

2. What did the rabbit tell his friends every time?

3. Why did the rabbit give his picture to the bugs?

Create and Share

Paint a picture. Look at other children's paintings. Tell what you like about each one.

Explore

Look at some books and find a painting that you like.

Straw Painting

by Rose Fiorentino

Straw painting is fun. To make a straw painting, you will need:

straws

paints and brush

paper

dishes

newspaper

First put some papers down where you will work. Mix some paint with some drops of water.

Next put some drops of paint on your paper.

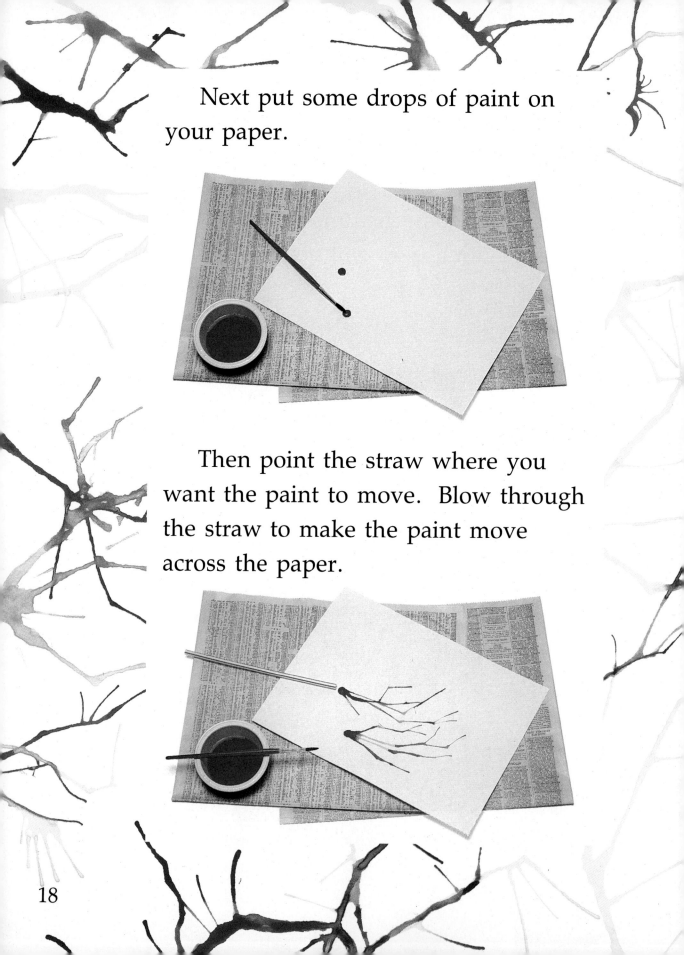

Then point the straw where you want the paint to move. Blow through the straw to make the paint move across the paper.

Add other colors of paint. Blow
through the straw some more.

You can see how the colors mix
and make other colors. What does
your straw painting tell you about
mixing colors?

Paints

When I put YELLOW
Paint on RED,
The colors change
To ORANGE instead.

And, mixing BLUE
And RED, I get
A pretty shade
of VIOLET.

Another trick
That I have seen:
YELLOW and BLUE
Turn into GREEN.

There's magic when
My colors mix.
It's fun to watch them
Doing tricks.

—Ilo Orleans

Think About It

1. What does "Straw Painting" say you need for this kind of painting?

2. How is a straw painting like or not like the painting the rabbit did in "The Picture"?

3. Tell how "Straw Painting" and "Paints" are the same.

Create and Share

Make a color book. Tell a friend how you made it.

Explore

Pick a color. Look for things that have that color. See how many you can find.

Wishing Well

Star light, star bright,
First star I see tonight,
I wish I may, I wish I might,
Have the wish I wish tonight.

The Three Wishes

Grimm fairy tale
retold by Nora Brooks Blakely

Long ago there was an old man and an old woman who lived in a little house. The house was falling down. The man and woman had little to eat.

One day the old man got up and said to his wife, "Today I must go cut down trees."

The old woman said, "Well, work as you must, but be back before the day must go to sleep. Bring us something to eat too."

"Yes, I will," he said. With that, he was off to cut down trees.

He worked and worked. When he stopped, he had cut down seven trees.

"I will cut down one more tree," said the old man.

"Stop that! Stop that! Stop that, I say!"

The man looked up. A little dwarf with big feet was up in the tree.

"Hello," said the old man. "Why are you up in that tree?"

"I live in here," said the little dwarf.

The dwarf came down out of the tree. He said, "If you don't cut down my home, I will give you three wishes!"

"Three wishes? Very well. I will not cut down your tree," said the old man. Then he waved good-bye to the dwarf and went home. He did not think about the three wishes.

When the old man got home, his wife said, "What did you bring us to eat?"

"I have nothing for us to eat," said the old man. Then he sat down. He did not think of the dwarf. He did not think of the trees. He did think of something to eat.

"I wish I had a fish," said the man.

Pop!

A big fish sat at his feet.

"Oh my!" said the old man.

"Oh my!" said the old woman.
"Who put this fish here?"

"I think the little dwarf did it,"
the old man said.

"What dwarf?" she asked.

So the old man told his wife
about the dwarf and the wishes.

"You get three wishes and you ask for a fish?" she said. "You must be mad! I wish that fish was on your nose."

Pop!

The fish was on the man's nose!

"Oh, no! Now the fish is on my nose!" said the old man.

"And we have just one wish left,"
said the old woman.

The old man looked at the old woman.
She looked back at him. There was just
one thing to do.

"I wish this fish was back at my feet,"
said the old man.

Pop!

The fish was back at his feet. So they
cooked the fish. Then they sat down
and ate it. Yes, they did! A fish is good
to eat. But it is not good on your nose!

Think About It

1. Do you think the old man and the old woman liked their wishes? Why or why not?

2. What did the old man really need to wish for?

3. What about this tale is real?

4. What about this tale is not real?

Create and Share

Draw a picture of something you wish for. See if a friend can guess your wish.

Explore

Read a book about wishes.

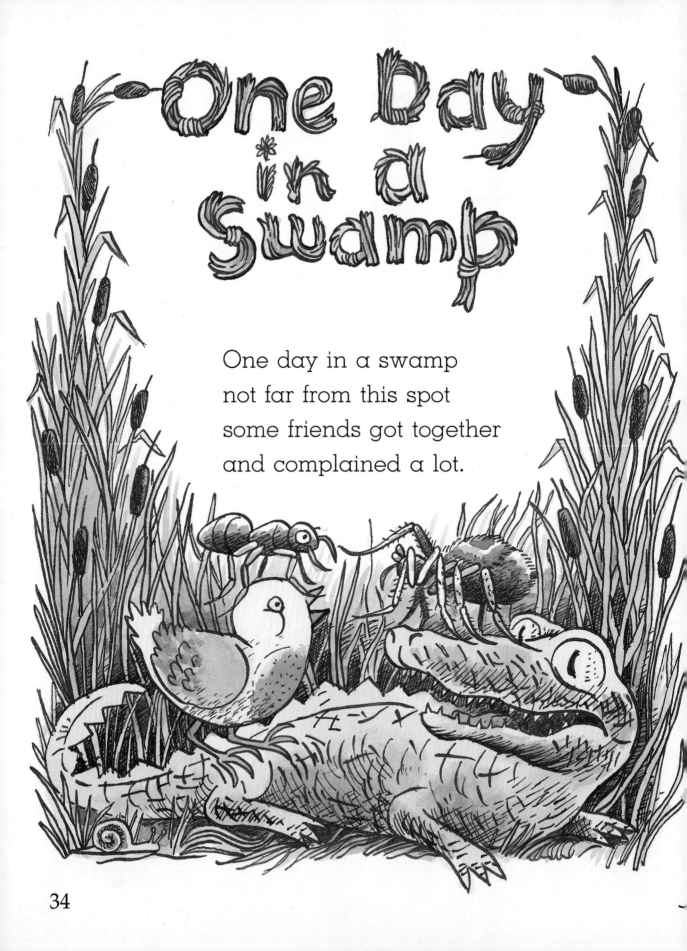

One Day in a Swamp

One day in a swamp
not far from this spot
some friends got together
and complained a lot.

One was an alligator
sitting on a log.
"Nobody likes alligators.
I wish I was a dog."

One was a spider
hanging in a tree.
"A spider's life is dull.
I wish I was a bee."

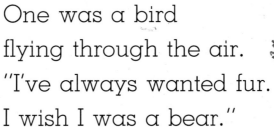

One was a bird
flying through the air.
"I've always wanted fur.
I wish I was a bear."

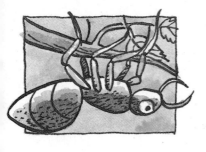

One was an ant
Swinging from a twig.
"Ants are so small.
I wish I was a pig."

Up from the water
popped a tiny fish.
"I know the magic words.
I'll see you get your wish."

"Boola! Boola! Boola!"
They heard the fish say.
He said it once more.
They all had their way.

One day in a swamp
not far from this spot
some friends got together
and complained a lot.

One was a dog
sitting on a log
sinking in a bog.

One was a bee
stuck in a web
high in a tree.

One was a bear
falling

through the air
to who knows where.

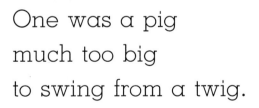

One was a pig
much too big
to swing from a twig.

—Joan Roth Schmeichel

Wishes for Hattie

by Dick Gackenbach

"Your mother has funny feet," said Hattie Rabbit to Little Chicken.

"They are good for scratching up worms," said Little Chicken.

"I wish," said Hattie, "my mother had feet like that."

"Your mother has a very long neck," said Hattie to Little Giraffe.

"She can reach the tender leaves at the tops of trees," said Little Giraffe.

"I wish," said Hattie, "my mother had a neck that long."

"That is some nose your mother has," said Hattie to Little Elephant.

"It is great for taking a bath," said Little Elephant.

Hattie watched Little Elephant get his bath.

"Wow!" she said. "I wish my mother had a nose like that."

"Goodness," thought Hattie. "What if my wishes came true?"

She thought some more. "If my mother had feet like Mrs. Chicken," she said, "I would have to eat worms. Ugh, I hate worms.

"If she had a neck like Mrs. Giraffe, I would have to climb on a ladder to give her a kiss.

"If she had a nose like Mrs. Elephant, one sneeze would blow the roof right off our house."

"No," said Hattie, "I take my wishes back. I want my mother the way she is, warm, soft, and furry."

Think About It

1. How did the animals in the poem "One Day in a Swamp" feel after they got their wishes?

2. In "Wishes for Hattie," why did Hattie take her wishes back?

3. What can you tell people about making wishes?

Create and Share

Draw a picture to show Hattie's mother if Hattie got her wishes.

Explore

Ask some friends what they wish. See how many wish for the same thing.

Home Sweet Home

If you were an animal,
      what would you be?
Where would you go,
      and what would you see?

When you make your home,
      where will you be?
On the ground, by the pond,
      or up in a tree?

The Town Mouse and The Country Mouse

Aesop fable
retold by Sherry Litwack

A Town Mouse went to see an old friend in the country.

"Have a little something to eat," said the Country Mouse. "I don't have much, but you are welcome to what I have."

"Thank you," said the Town Mouse. "You are very kind."

"It is nice here in the country," said the Town Mouse, "but you must come to town with me. There are many things to see there."

"Well, I am happy here," said the Country Mouse, "but I'd like to see your home in town."

"Let's go!" said the Town Mouse.

So they walked all the way to town.
The Town Mouse and the Country Mouse
went inside a big house.

"Come here," said the Town Mouse.

They came to a table filled with good
things to eat.

The Country Mouse said, "This is
great! I can see why you like it here."

"Yes," said the Town Mouse. "This
is the best way to live!"

Just then something huge ran into the room. It jumped up on the table.

"Come on!" said the Town Mouse. "Let's get out of here! Run! Run for your life!"

The Town Mouse and the Country Mouse ran as fast as their little feet could go.

"What was that huge thing?" asked the Country Mouse.

"That was a cat," said the Town Mouse. "Cats like to eat mice."

"They do?" said the Country Mouse. "I think it is time for me to go home. This town life is not for me."

"Well, I guess it is not for everyone," said the Town Mouse.

So the Country Mouse went back
to the country where she could eat
what little she had in peace. And she
never went into town again.

Think About It

1. Why did the Town Mouse want the Country Mouse to come to her home?

2. How did each mouse come to see that her home was best?

3. What is good about life in town?

4. What is good about country life?

Create and Share

Draw a picture of where a friend lives. Tell what is good about where your friend lives.

Explore

Look at some books. Which are about towns? Which are about the country?

Animals at Home

by Tess Lindy

Animals live in different places.
Some animal homes are in the ground.
Some animal homes are in the water.
Some animal homes are in the woods.

Look at the ground. Do you see
some animal homes?

Ants make nests under the ground.
Rabbits look for holes in the ground
where they can sleep or hide. Foxes
make a den in the ground. Foxes take
care of their babies in the den.

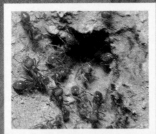

Look at the water. Do you see some animal homes?

A frog sits by a brook. A fish swims in the pond. Water bugs live in ponds and brooks too.

Look in the woods. Do you see some animal homes?

Birds make nests in trees. Bees make nests in trees too. Squirrels play hide-and-seek in the trees. They make their home there.

There are animal homes in many different places. Can you think of other places where animals live?

Think About It

1. Why do different animals make homes in different places?

2. What animal homes have you seen?

3. You can live in the ground, in the water, or in a tree. Where will you live? Why?

Create and Share

Draw an animal and show where it lives. Tell what you know about the animal. Tell why this is a good home for the animal.

Explore

Read about an animal and its home.

The Frog in the Bog

by Elsie S. Santos

There was a frog by the name of
Croaker Dan. He made his home under
some trees. It was a very good home.
There was a pond next to it. Croaker
Dan could always get food there.

Croaker Dan was like other frogs
in many ways, but there was one thing
different about him. He was never
happy with the way things were.

When it was warm, he said, "I hate it when it is warm." When it was cold, he said, "I hate it when it is cold."

Croaker Dan was not happy with his home. He wished that he lived in a different place.

"My friend Croaker Joe has a nice home," he thought. "He lives by a brook. He can jump in any time he wants. I wish I lived by a brook."

So Croaker Dan put some food in his sack. Then he went to look for a brook.

He jumped up the hill and down the hill. He jumped through the woods. At last he came to a brook.

He made his home by the brook. Then he jumped into the water.

"Brrrrr . . . This water is cold! I'm not staying here," he said.

"My friend Croaker Jill has a nice home," he thought. "She lives on a farm with lots of horses, cows, and dogs! I wish I had a home like hers." So he went to look for a farm.

Again he jumped through the woods. He jumped up the hill and down the hill.

At last, he came to a farm. The farm had horses, cows, and dogs. He made his home by some rocks and went to sleep.

When he woke up, a dog was looking at him. The dog was mad at Croaker Dan!

Croaker Dan jumped away as fast as he could. "That does it. I am not going to stay here with that dog!"

He looked and looked again. Then he saw a cranberry bog. There were so many red cranberries. The bog looked nice and wet too.

"I will make a home here," Croaker Dan said.

He sat down in the bog. He was
about to take a nap when a big noise
made him jump.

Cranberries were falling on him.
He looked up and saw a machine.
The machine was coming at him.
It was picking up the cranberries.

Croaker Dan moved very fast. He jumped just in time. Then he saw a second machine coming at him. He jumped out of the bog.

"I got out of there just in time," he said.

Croaker Dan thought about all the homes he had made. Then he said, "I hope my little home under the trees is still there! I guess there will always be something about everything that I do not like. But from now on, I will be happy with what I have."

Croaker Dan went back to his home under the trees. It was late the next day when he got there. For the first time, Croaker Dan was happy with everything just the way it was.

Think About It

1. Why did Croaker Dan look for a new home?

2. Tell about each of the homes that Croaker Dan lived in.

3. How is Croaker Dan like the Country Mouse?

4. Think of places you might like to live. Tell where and why.

Create and Share

Be Croaker Dan. Tell about one place you lived.

Explore

See what you can find out about frogs.

Make new friends
But keep the old;
One is silver and the
Other is gold.

New Friends
and Old

The Mixed-Up Lunch

by Bernard Wiseman

Boris the Bear said to Billy and Sally, "Thanks for asking us to lunch. It's nice to make new friends."

Morris the Moose said, "Billy and Sally aren't **new** friends. They're **old** friends."

Boris asked, "How can they be **old** friends? They just moved here."

Morris laughed. "Billy is six years old. Sally is seven years old. That makes them **old** friends."

Billy and Sally thought that was funny.

"We're happy that you could come to lunch," said Billy.

"Yes," said Sally, "Mom said it was a good way to make friends."

"Mom?" said Morris. "Who is he?"

Boris said, "A mom isn't a he. A mom is a she."

"Yes," said Sally. "A mom is a she and I am a she."

Billy said, "Sally is a she and I am a he."

Boris said, "And I am a he!"

Morris thought hard and said, "I am a me!"

"Yes," said Boris. "You're a me and a he."

Morris asked, "Am I a Me-He?"

"No!" said Boris. "You're not a Me-Me! No! No! I mean, you're not a Me-He!"

"Then what am I?" asked Morris.

"You're a moose that can mix me up," said Boris.

Sally said, "Let's eat lunch now!"

"We're having hot dogs for lunch," said Billy.

"Hot dogs!" yelled Morris. "I couldn't eat a hot dog. I don't think I could eat a cold dog. I like dogs."

"A hot dog isn't a real dog," said
Sally. "Look, this is a hot dog."

"Oh," said Morris. He took a bite.
"Hot dogs are good. Do you ever have
hot cats for lunch?"

Billy and Sally laughed and laughed.
"Morris, you're a silly moose."

"Now that we're done eating, let's read a book," said Billy.

"I'll read," said Boris. "Jack and Jill went up the hill."

"Why did they go up the hill?" asked Morris.

"To get water," said Boris.

"Water is in lakes or ponds," said Morris. "Water isn't on hills."

"Stop! Stop!" said Boris. "Water
was on this hill. Just let me read. Jack
and hill went up the Jill. No! I mean
Jack and Jill went up the Jill. No!
Forget it. I'll read a different book.
I'll read *The Three Little Pigs*."

"Wait," said Morris. "Pigs aren't
little. They're big. You mean
The Three Big Pigs."

"No!" said Boris. "I don't mean
The Three Big Pigs! I mean
The Three Little Bigs! No! You mix
me up so much that I don't know what
I mean."

Sally said, "I think we're done reading."

"Yes," said Boris, "we have to go."

"Now that we have met, I hope you'll come to our house again," said Billy.

"I'll come back," said Morris. "Next time we'll have some hot cats for lunch. Then we'll read *The Three Little Jack and Jills*."

"Oh, let's just go home now," said Boris.

Think About It

1. Why do you think Morris and Boris are old friends?

2. Why did Sally and Billy ask Morris and Boris to lunch?

3. What funny things did Morris do?

4. Tell why this story is not real.

Create and Share

My friend and I like to _____. Draw a picture that shows what you and your friend like to do.

Explore

Read other Morris and Boris books by Bernard Wiseman.

A New Friend

They've taken in the furniture;
I watched them carefully.
I wondered, "Will there be a child
Just right to play with me?"

So I peeked through the garden fence
(I couldn't wait to see).
I found the little boy next door
Was peeking back at me.

—Marjorie Allen Anderson

The Stranger

by Tony Johnston

"Hey, you," said a strange voice.

"Hey, who?" said Odd Jobs.

"You with the funny hat. I have a job I don't think you can do."

"What will you give me if I can?" asked Odd Jobs.

"I'll give you a pair of sunglasses and seven fish," said the stranger.

Odd Jobs said, "I always take cold cash, not cold fish."

"This job is different," said the stranger. "Take it or leave it."

"I'll take it. What's the job?"

"Keep me company till I find a friend. I'm new on the block."

"I don't keep strangers company," said Odd Jobs.

"I'm Floyd," said the stranger. "Now I'm not a stranger."

Odd Jobs did keep Floyd company.
Floyd walked across a fence. He walked
across it in one minute.

"Come on," Floyd grinned. "Keep
me company."

Odd Jobs walked across the fence.
He almost fell. It took five minutes,
but he stuck with Floyd.

Floyd climbed up a tree. He climbed to the top and waved. "Odd Jobs, hurry up. Keep me company."

Odd Jobs climbed up and up and up. He didn't want to look down. He passed lots of green leaves. He looked green. But he stuck with Floyd.

Next Floyd grabbed a pail and jumped
into the pond. He sank in mud up to
his knees. "Come on," he called.
"Keep me company."

"Yuk," said Odd Jobs.

"How do you like this mud?" Floyd
asked.

"I said yuk," Odd Jobs said again.
But he stuck with Floyd.

Then Floyd saw a frog. He saw
two frogs. He saw lots of frogs.
Squish. Squish. Squish. He walked
out to catch them. Floyd put the frogs
in his pail.

"Hurry up before they are all gone,"
Floyd yelled. "Your job is to keep me
company."

"Oh, right," Odd Jobs said, walking
in the mud. "Yuk."

"Take this," Floyd said, giving him
a big croaker.

Odd Jobs didn't know what to say.
So he said, "Thanks."

Flop, flop, the big croaker jumped
out of his hands and down Floyd's shirt.
Floyd yelled. And jumped. And danced.
He ran all over the place. Odd Jobs
stuck right with him.

Then Floyd grabbed the frog and sat down. So did Odd Jobs. They laughed and laughed till they had no laughs left.

"You're doing a bad job," Floyd told Odd Jobs.

"I'm doing great," Odd Jobs said. "I'm sticking right with you."

"But I have to find a friend."

"Oh, right," said Odd Jobs. "Well, you do crazy things. You walk on fences and climb up trees. You walk in the mud to catch frogs. You're so crazy that I really like you. I'll be your friend."

"You will?" Floyd asked.

"Yes, I will." Odd Jobs grinned.

"Great. Let's get the sunglasses and the fish."

"Forget it," Odd Jobs said. "I don't take pay from new friends."

Think About It

1. Do you think the children in the poem "A New Friend" will be friends? Why or why not?

2. In "The Stranger," what was the job Odd Jobs took?

3. Why was the job hard for Odd Jobs?

4. What did you find out about meeting new friends?

Create and Share

List things you can do to make a new friend. Read your list to the class.

Explore

Read more about Odd Jobs in books by Tony Johnston.

The eensy weensy spider
went up the water spout.
Down came the rain and
washed the spider out.

Out came the sun and
dried up all the rain.
And the eensy weensy spider
went up the spout again.

Wind and
Rain

The Surprise

by Arnold Lobel

It was October. The leaves had fallen off the trees. They were lying on the ground.

"I will go to Toad's house," said Frog. "I will rake all of the leaves that have fallen on his lawn. Toad will be surprised."

Frog took a rake out of the garden shed.

Toad looked out of his window.

"These messy leaves have covered everything," said Toad. He took a rake out of the closet. "I will run over to Frog's house. I will rake all of his leaves. Frog will be very pleased."

Frog ran through the woods so that
Toad would not see him.

Toad ran through the high grass
so that Frog would not see him.

Frog came to Toad's house. He
looked in the window.

"Good," said Frog. "Toad is out.
He will never know who raked his
leaves."

Toad got to Frog's house. He looked in the window.

"Good," said Toad. "Frog is not home. He will never guess who raked his leaves."

Frog worked and worked. He raked
the leaves into a pile. Soon Toad's lawn
was clean. Frog picked up his rake and
started home.

Toad pushed and pulled on the rake.
He raked the leaves into a pile. Soon
there was not a single leaf in Frog's
front yard. Toad took his rake and
started home.

A wind came. It blew across the land. The pile of leaves that Frog had raked for Toad blew everywhere. The pile of leaves that Toad had raked for Frog blew everywhere.

When Frog got home, he said, "Tomorrow I will clean up the leaves that are all over my own lawn. How surprised Toad must be!"

When Toad got home, he said,
"Tomorrow I will get to work and rake
all of my own leaves. How surprised
Frog must be!"

That night Frog and Toad were both
happy when they each turned out the
light and went to bed.

Think About It

1. How do you know Frog and Toad are good friends?

2. How does the wind surprise Frog and Toad?

3. What can Frog and Toad do so that the leaves will not blow away the next time?

Create and Share

Draw two pictures. Show a surprise someone gave you and a surprise you gave someone else.

Explore

Look for books by Arnold Lobel about Frog and Toad.

The Rain Puddle

by Adelaide Holl

Plump Hen was picking and pecking in the meadow grass.

"Cluck, cluck! Cluck, cluck!" she said softly to herself.

All at once, she came to a rain puddle.

"Dear me!" she cried. "A plump little hen has fallen into the water!"

Away she ran calling, "Awk, awk! Cut-a-cut! Cut-a-cut! Cut-a-cut!"

Turkey was eating corn in the barnyard.

"Come at once!" called Plump Hen. "A hen is in the rain puddle!"

Away went Turkey to see for himself.

"Gobble-obble-obble!" he cried when he looked in. "It is not a plump hen. It is a big, bright turkey gobbler!"

Pig was crunching red apples in the orchard. He heard the news. Off he waddled to take a look.

"Snort, snort! Oink, oink! They are both wrong," Pig said to himself. "It is a beautiful, fat pig that has fallen into the rain puddle. I must get help at once!"

Curly Sheep was nibbling sweet clover in the pasture, and Cow was softly chewing her cud under a shady tree.

"What is going on?" they said to one another. "Let us go and see."

They found all the other animals crowded around the puddle together.

"A whole barnyard full of animals
has fallen into the water," they all
exclaimed. "We must run for help!"

While all the animals were running
about in great excitement, the sun came
out. The sun shone warm and bright.
It dried the rain puddle all up.

Plump Hen stopped running around
in circles and cried, "Awk, awk!
Cut, cut! Look! The animals have all
climbed out safely!"

Away she went to pick and peck in
the meadow grass.

"Gobble-obble-obble! So they have!"
agreed Turkey. Off he went to eat corn
in the barnyard.

"You are quite right," snorted Pig.
He waddled off to crunch red apples
in the orchard.

Curly Sheep said, "Baaaa, baaaa," and went back to nibble sweet clover in the pasture.

"Moooo, moooo!" said Cow. "All of the animals escaped!" Off she went to find a shady tree and to chew her cud.

Wise Old Owl looked down from a tree above and chuckled to himself.

Making a Weather Chart

by Cynthia C. Nye

Look out your window. What is the weather like? What will you wear and do in today's weather?

Think about what you might do on a windy day. Think about what you would wear on a cold, rainy day.

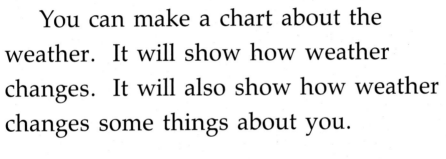

You can make a chart about the weather. It will show how weather changes. It will also show how weather changes some things about you.

You will need these things to make a weather chart.

ruler

crayons

paper

1. First, fold your paper in half. Then fold it in half again. Draw a line along each fold in the paper.

2. Now write these words in the spaces across the top of your paper. Draw a line under each word.

Day	Sky	What We Do	What We Wear

3. Write the days of the week down your paper under the word **day**. Then draw a line under each day. Make each line go all the way across the paper.

Day	Sky	What We Do	What We Wear
Monday			
Tuesday			
Wednesday			
Thursday			
Friday			
Saturday			
Sunday			

4. Find today on your chart. Move one box to the right. Draw today's weather in the box.

Day	Sky	What We Do	What We Wear
Monday	☼		
Tuesday			
Wednesday			

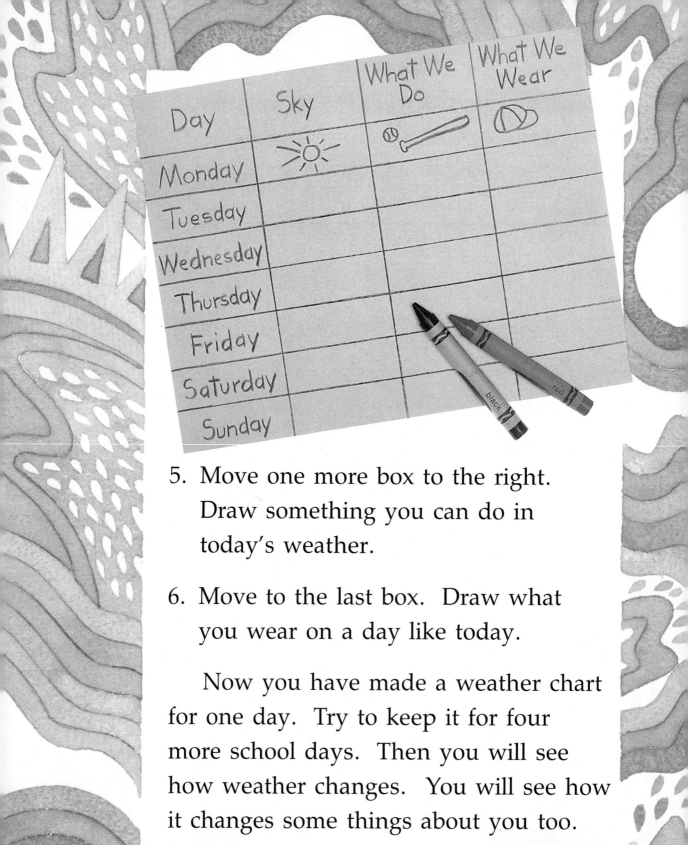

Day	Sky	What We Do	What We Wear
Monday			
Tuesday			
Wednesday			
Thursday			
Friday			
Saturday			
Sunday			

5. Move one more box to the right. Draw something you can do in today's weather.

6. Move to the last box. Draw what you wear on a day like today.

Now you have made a weather chart for one day. Try to keep it for four more school days. Then you will see how weather changes. You will see how it changes some things about you too.

Think About It

1. How does a change in the weather change what you do outside?

2. How does it change what you wear?

3. How might "The Surprise" be different if Frog and Toad made a weather chart?

Create and Share

Make a weather chart. Use the steps in your book to help you.

Explore

Read, watch, and listen for news about the weather.

Toys, Toys, Toys

*Try saying this tongue twister
three times fast:*

Tommy's toy trumpet
toodles terrible tunes.

Who's Talking, Elena?

by Bonnie Brescia

Narrator

Mr. Nelson, a man

Elena, a girl

Bossy, a stuffed toy cow

Lickety-Split, a skateboard

Booker, a book

Dizzy Izzy, a puzzle

Narrator: In the city, there is a toy shop where toys talk. Some people don't think that toys can talk. Do you? Let's watch as a girl named Elena walks into the shop to buy a toy.

Mr. Nelson: (*smiling*) Welcome to Nelson's Toy Shop. May I help you?

Elena: Hello. My name is Elena. I came to buy a toy. But I don't know what I want.

Mr. Nelson: Well, Elena, I have all kinds of toys in the shop. Why don't you look over there?

Narrator: Elena walks over to look at the toys. Suddenly she hears a strange voice. Someone is yelling, but she can't see anyone.

Bossy: (*very loud*) You there! What are you doing in this toy shop?

Elena: (*whisper*) Who, me?

Bossy: (*loud*) Yes, you. What's your name? What do you think you're doing here?

Elena: My name is Elena. I'm shopping for a new toy. Who's talking? Where are you?

Bossy: I'm over here. I'm the stuffed toy cow. They call me Bossy. I tell everyone what to do! That's why they call me Bossy.

Narrator: Suddenly a skateboard starts to talk very fast.

Lickety-Split: (*very fast*) Hello, hello, hello. Zoom, zoom. Hello.

Elena: Hello. Who are you?

Lickety-Split: My friends call me Lickety-Split. I'm a fast skateboard.

Bossy: (*loud*) Shh, Lickety-Split! I was talking to Elena. Now, Elena, tell me what you're shopping for. I will tell you where to find it.

Elena: I don't know. There are so many toys here. I just don't know which one to pick.

Dizzy Izzy: It's a trick,

Which to pick.

Look and see.

Why not me?

Elena: Who said that?

Dizzy Izzy: Way up here,

Elena, dear.

Next to Lizzy.

My name's Izzy.

Lickety-Split: I call him Dizzy Izzy.

He's a puzzle. He talks like one.

Booker: Hey, Elena. My name is Booker. Can you read?

Elena: Yes, I can read. Why?

Booker: Well, I'm a storybook. And I don't know what my stories are about. Would you read me before you go home?

Elena: I think I could read one story.

Booker: Oh, thank you!

Elena: (*reading*) A long time ago a little girl was walking in the woods. She came to a house. She looked inside and saw a little chair, a big chair, and . . .

Lickety-Split: (*yelling*) Elena! Let's go for a ride! Hop on!

Elena: I'm reading now, Lickety. Can you wait till I'm done?

Lickety-Split: Wait? I don't know how to wait. Zoom, zoom. I'm off!

Bossy: It's getting late, Elena. I think you have to pick a toy before the shop closes. I know I would look very nice on your bed.

Booker: (*yelling*) Wait! Wait! What about the little girl and the chairs? How does the story end? Read some more! Please take me home and read me.

Dizzy Izzy: Pick me, pick me!
You can see
I want to go,
So don't say no.

Lickety-Split: Forget it, Izzy. Hop on, Elena. I'll take you home. Let's go. Go! Go! Go!

Mr. Nelson: Elena, I have to close the shop now. Do you need any help?

Elena: Thanks, Mr. Nelson, but I think I have more help than I need. I'm still talking it over.

Mr. Nelson: (*looking mixed-up*) Talking it over? You're all alone!

Elena: Umm, I mean I am still thinking it over.

Mr. Nelson: Well, please hurry.

Narrator: Mr. Nelson walks away. Elena turns back to Bossy, Dizzy Izzy, Lickety-Split, and Booker.

Elena: You are all very nice toys. Bossy, you would look nice in my room. Lickety-Split, it would be fun to go for a ride. Dizzy Izzy, I like the way you talk. You would be a fun puzzle to have.

Bossy, Dizzy Izzy, Lickety-Split: Thanks! We like you too, Elena.

Elena: I know you all want to come home with me. But I can take just one of you home.

Booker: What about me, Elena?

Elena: You may come home with me. When I read your stories, I will think of Bossy, Lickety-Split, and Dizzy Izzy. That way it will be like taking all of you home.

Mr. Nelson: Elena, what a great book!

Elena: Yes, Mr. Nelson, I'm very happy with Booker.

Narrator: Elena waved good-bye to the toys. Mr. Nelson didn't know why Elena was waving. But all the toys smiled and waved back.

Think About It

1. Why was it hard for Elena to pick a toy?

2. Why did Elena pick Booker?

3. Which toy did you think Elena would take home? Why?

4. Tell which toy you would pick and why.

Create and Share

Draw a picture of one of your toys. Tell what it would say to you if it could talk.

Explore

Look for other plays to read.

TOYS

·CATALOG·

by Marc Brown

Shopping in a catalog is fun. It is a great way to look at things you might want to buy too.

A toy catalog tells you about different toys and shows you pictures of them.

Pretend it is your friend's birthday. Look at the next two pages from a toy catalog. What present would you pick for your friend?

Bounce Back

Play catch alone. Throw the ball and watch it bounce back to you. Don't forget to catch it!

Press·A·Pet

Talk to the animals and they talk back to you! Learn how to care for seven favorite pets from the pets themselves.

Streaker Sneaker

Just press the magic power button and go. Streaker Sneakers come in all sizes. (Colors — red or blue)

Magic Power Button

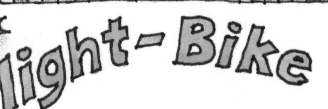

Flight-Bike

Ride it! Fly it! Great new bike for those who want to get there in a hurry.

Jack·in·the·Hat

Poof! Up pops Jack in a puff of smoke, and each time with a new trick for you.

U.F.O. Kite

Easy to fly. It looks like a real U.F.O. with its blinking lights and beeping sounds.

Sal and the Toy Fair

by Alex and Esther Cervantes

Sal needed an idea. There was going to be a toy fair at school. All his friends were making toys to show at the fair. Sal wanted to make the best toy of all. He wanted to make something that all his friends could play with.

"What can I make for the toy fair?" Sal asked his father.

"You could make a boat," said Father.

"Mark made paper boats," said Sal. "He showed me how to sail them. I want something different."

"You'll think of something," said Father.

Sal thought and thought.

"What can I make for the toy fair?" Sal asked his mother.

"You could make a kite," said Mother.

"Kim made a green kite with a long red tail," said Sal. "We flew it after school today. I need something different."

"You'll think of something," said Mother.

Sal went to his room to think.

"Music will help me come up with a toy idea," he thought. He turned on his radio.

Music from the radio filled the air. Sal tapped his foot to the beat. He could hear the horns hoot. He could hear the drums bang. The radio made Sal want to play music, and it gave him an idea.

"Oh," thought Sal. "I know just what to make for the toy fair!"

"I have a great idea for the toy fair, Dad! May I have an old pan and some lids?" Sal asked.

"I think I can find something for you," said his father. "What are you going to make?"

"You'll see," said Sal. "May I have some spoons and a jar of rice too?"

"Yes," said his father, "but we'll need these things back after the fair."

Then Sal went to find Mother.

"Mother, I have a great idea for the toy fair! May I have some yarn for my toy?" asked Sal.

"Yes, Sal. I have some red yarn left over from a hat. What are you going to make?" asked Mother.

"You'll see," said Sal.

The next day Sal's friends came to his house.

"A pan and lids," said Jake. "What can you make from those things?"

"You'll see," said Sal.

"Spoons and a jar of rice," said Jenny. "What can you make from them?"

"You'll see," said Sal.

Sal showed his friends what to do. They tied some of the spoons with yarn. Then Mark hit these spoons with another spoon.

Kim shook the jar of rice. Jenny banged the lids. Jake took two spoons and hit the pan.

"This is fun!" they said.

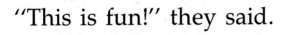

"Sal has made a toy band with kitchen things," said Mark.

"We all can be in the band," said Kim. "We'll play for everyone at the toy fair."

And that's just what they did!

Think About It

1. Which toy would you pick from the "Toy Catalog" for your own? Why?

2. Why do people use catalogs?

3. In "Sal and the Toy Fair," what did Sal have to do?

4. Why was a toy band a good idea?

Create and Share

Make a list of toys. Find out which toy everyone likes best.

Explore

Look through some toy catalogs. Look to see what the catalogs tell you about the toys.

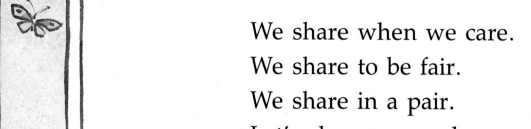

We share when we care.
We share to be fair.
We share in a pair.
Let's share everywhere.

Sharing

Mushroom in the Rain

*Russian folktale retold
by Mirra Ginsburg*

One day an ant was caught in the rain.

"Where can I hide?" he wondered.

He saw a little mushroom peeking out of the ground in a clearing, and he hid under it. He sat there, waiting for the rain to stop. But the rain came down and came down.

The sun looked out from behind the clouds. And everyone came out from under the mushroom, bright and merry.

The ant looked at his neighbors. "How could this be? At first there was barely room under the mushroom just for me, and in the end all five of us were able to sit under it."

"Qua-ha-ha! Qua-ha-ha!" laughed
a fat green frog sitting on top of the
mushroom.

"Qua-ha-ha!" said the frog. "Don't
you know what happens to a mushroom
in the rain?"

And he hopped away, still laughing.

The ant, the butterfly, the mouse, the bird, and the rabbit looked at each other. Then they looked at the mushroom. And suddenly they knew why there was room enough under the mushroom for them all.

Do you know?

Can you guess what happens to a mushroom when it rains?

It **grows!**

Think About It

1. What did the animals do when it started to rain?

2. Why do you think the rabbit was happy that the animals shared?

3. Why was there room for all the animals under the mushroom?

4. How do you stay dry in the rain?

Create and Share
Write about something you shared with a friend. Read it to the class.

Explore
Find a good book to share with a friend.

What Mary Jo Shared

by Janice May Udry

Every day Mary Jo's class had sharing time. Mary Jo never shared anything. She was too shy.

Almost every day her teacher, Miss Willet, would say, "And Mary Jo, do you have something to share?"

Mary Jo always shook her head and looked at the floor.

"Why don't you ever share anything?"
her friend Jenny asked.

"I will some day," said Mary Jo.
"I just don't want to yet."

Mary Jo really did want to share,
but she was very shy.

One morning it was raining hard.
When Mary Jo woke up, she saw the rain.

"I'll share my new umbrella," thought
Mary Jo.

She dressed and ate breakfast. Then she put on her new pink coat and got her pink umbrella.

Mary Jo walked to school in the rain. At school, she shook the water from her umbrella. Then Mary Jo went in. When she got to her classroom, she saw a lot of umbrellas. They were all sizes and colors.

"Almost everyone in my room has an umbrella too," thought Mary Jo. "I guess that isn't a good thing to share after all."

So when Miss Willet said, "And Mary Jo, do you have something to share?" Mary Jo shook her head and looked at the floor.

The next week Mary Jo and her brother caught a grasshopper.

"I'll share the grasshopper!" thought Mary Jo.

She put the grasshopper in a jar and went to school. When she walked into her classroom, she heard a girl say, "Jimmy's got **six** grasshoppers in a jar!"

Mary Jo thought about her one grasshopper.

"I guess I will not share my grasshopper after all," thought Mary Jo.

So when Miss Willet said, "And Mary Jo, do you have something to share?" Mary Jo shook her head and looked at the floor.

Mary Jo really wanted to share something that no one in the class had shared. It got so she couldn't think of anything else.

"What can I share?" she thought over and over.

Her father came home. "Did you share something at school today, Mary Jo?" he asked her.

Mary Jo said, "Not yet."

Then suddenly, Mary Jo thought of something!

"Can you go to school with me tomorrow?" she asked her father.

"Tomorrow? Why, yes, I think I can," said her father.

"Good!" said Mary Jo. "Then you can hear me share something!"

"All right," said her father, "I'll be there! What are you going to share?"

"Wait and see," said Mary Jo.

Mary Jo and her father went to school the next morning.

Mary Jo went up to Miss Willet and said, "I have something to share today."

"Fine," said Miss Willet. "You may share with us first this morning." Then she said hello to Mary Jo's father.

When it was sharing time, Mary Jo got up from her chair.

She smiled and said, "This morning I have brought my **father** to share!"

All the children turned to look at Mary Jo's father.

"This is my father, Mr. William Wood. He has a wife and three children.

"My father is a teacher. He likes to read a lot, and he writes quite a bit too. He knows how to sail boats. He likes to go fishing too.

"When my father was little, he was a bad boy sometimes," said Mary Jo.

"What did he do?" asked one of the children.

"Well, one time he locked his little brother out of the house. And one time he ate all the cake his mother had baked for a meeting," said Mary Jo. "Now my father will say a few words."

Mr. Wood smiled and told the children how nice it was to visit their class. Then Mary Jo and her father sat down.

Mary Jo was happy. At last she had shared something that no one else had thought of sharing.

Think About It

1. In "What Mary Jo Shared," what did Mary Jo want to do?

2. How did Mary Jo feel after she shared her father?

3. How was the way Mary Jo shared the same or different from the way the animals shared in "Mushroom in the Rain"?

Create and Share
Draw a picture of someone you would like to share. Tell about your picture.

Explore
Look for something you can share with your class.

Bear Tales

Try saying this tongue twister three times fast:

A big black bug
bit a big black bear.

Bears

by Kathleen S. Coleman

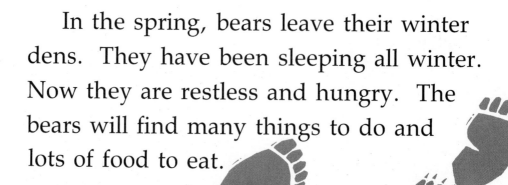

In the spring, bears leave their winter dens. They have been sleeping all winter. Now they are restless and hungry. The bears will find many things to do and lots of food to eat.

The bears begin to look for food.
They eat the new grass and flowers.
They will look for roots and berries also.
Bears use their long claws to pull bark
off a tree to get at the bugs. The bugs
living there are good to eat.

Bears like to wade in streams and lakes. They can swim very well. They catch fish to eat. Sometimes bear cubs play in the water.

If you were a bear, you could climb very well. Sometimes bears climb trees to get to beehives. The beehives have honey. Bears like honey very much. Bees can sting bears on their noses. Bees can't sting bears through their thick fur.

Before long, it is winter again. The bears go back to their dens. They have been eating and playing all summer. They will sleep day after day after day. When the warm spring air comes back, the bears will be happy to go outside to eat and play again.

Think About It

1. Tell three things about bears.

2. Where would you find a bear in the spring?

3. Where would you find a bear in the winter?

4. Why do you think bears sleep in the winter?

Create and Share

Draw a bear in the winter. Draw a bear in the spring. Tell what the bears are doing.

Explore

Read a book that tells about bears.

The Bear Went Over the Mountain

The bear went over the mountain,
The bear went over the mountain,
The bear went over the mountain,
To see what he could see.
To see what he could see,
To see what he could see.
The other side of the mountain,
The other side of the mountain,
The other side of the mountain
Was all that he could see.

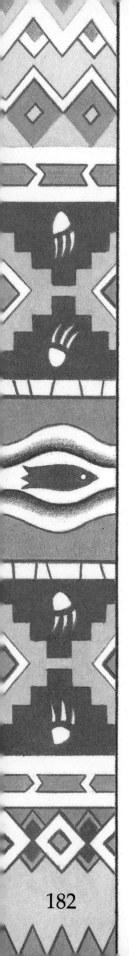

Why Bears Have Short Tails

Navajo legend
retold by Sandra Begay, a student
at Tuba City Boarding School

Fox was fishing in the river. When
he had ten fish, he put them on his back.
Then he walked off into the woods.

Bear saw Fox with the fish on his back.

"How come you have so many fish on your back? How are you fishing for those fish?"

Fox said, "It's easy. You sit on the ice and put your tail in the river. The fish catch onto your tail. When you get up, there will be a lot of fish just hanging on."

"Thanks," said Bear as he ran to the river.

Fox was laughing as he went through the woods with his ten fish. Bear didn't see him laughing.

Bear sat on the ice. He sat there a long time, waiting and waiting. He didn't feel any fish jumping onto his long tail. He could feel his tail getting very cold. It hurt.

After a long time, Bear said, "I can't feel my tail."

He got up and looked. It was true. His long tail had frozen and fallen off. All he had left was a very short tail.

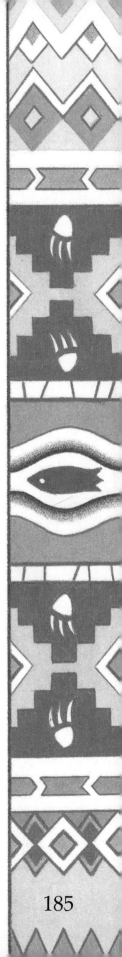

Bear was very mad at Fox. He gave up fishing and ran into the woods to look for Fox.

Fox was cooking his ten fish when Bear grabbed him.

Bear said, "You tricked me. My long and pretty tail froze and fell off. So now I'm taking you back to that river. I'll throw you in and let you freeze."

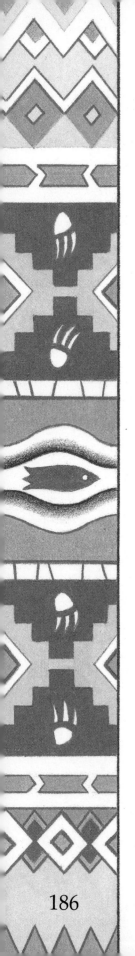

"No," Fox said. "Don't do that. If you let me go, I'll give you all my fish."

So Bear let Fox go. Bear ate all the fish. Then he warmed his short tail by Fox's fire.

Now all bears have short tails. That is how it happened.

Think About It

1. What do you think the bear in "The Bear Went Over the Mountain" thought he would see?

2. How is the fox in "Why Bears Have Short Tails" the same as or different from the fox in "Mushroom in the Rain"?

Create and Share
Write a story telling why you think mice have long tails.

Explore
Find another book that has a fox in it. Tell what the fox is like.

Good As New

by Barbara Douglass

I thought my grandpa could fix anything.

One morning last week he fixed the hose and the fence. Then he fixed my swing and my sandbox. He also fixed Yim Lee's fire engine and Carmen's wagon.

One day my cousin K.C. came to visit while Uncle Jonathan went to work. K.C. started crying as soon as my uncle rode away.

Nobody could make him happy, not even Grandpa. The only thing K.C. wanted was my bear. And I said, "Uh-uh. Nobody plays with my bear but me."

K.C. kicked the floor, and he cried some more.

Mom said, "Grady, do you think K.C. feels lonely because he didn't bring **his** bear?"

Then Dad said, "Do you think he might feel better, Son, if you just let him hold your bear?"

Grandpa didn't say anything. K.C. cried even harder until Yim Lee and Carmen grabbed their toys and went home. Grandpa grabbed his hat and went for a walk.

Before I could say, "Okay, you can **hold** him," K.C. grabbed my bear. But he didn't just hold him.

He dragged my bear around by the ears. Then he fed him peanut butter. Next he tried to feed him to the dog.

Dad made him stop.

Then K.C. dragged my bear outside where he sat on him. And he turned the hose on him.

Dad made him stop that too.

So K.C. buried my bear in the sand.

After K.C. went home, I dug up my bear.

Mom said, "Please, don't bring it into the house."

Dad said, "I'm sorry it's ruined, Son. I'll buy you a new one."

I said, "I don't want a new bear. I want this old one fixed. I want him the way he was before K.C. came."

Mom shook her head. Dad did too.

But Grandpa hung up his hat. He said, "Never you mind now, Grady. I can fix that bear so he'll be as good as new in no time."

Then he brought a big brown paper bag outside. We sat down.

Grandpa opened up his pocket knife!

I said, "**Wait** a minute. What's that for, Grandpa? Are you sure you can fix my bear?"

"Of course I can," he said to me. "Hold on here. Now pull so I can see to cut the stitches."

I held on and I pulled, but I didn't want to watch. Grandpa opened up my bear. Then he started pulling out the stuffing.

My bear's stomach went flat, the way mine feels when I'm hungry. His arms and legs wrinkled up too.

I said, "Grandpa, are you sure this is the right way to fix my bear?"

Grandpa just kept on working.

My bear's nose dropped, and his head flopped.

I covered up my eyes, and I said, "Grandpa! Are you sure?"

He said, "Never you mind now, Grady. We'll have this bear as good as new in no time."

In the kitchen, we made a sinkful of suds.

Grandpa scrubbed my bear. First he scrubbed the stomach. Then he scrubbed the arms and legs, and the neck and the nose. He even scrubbed the ears.

But he scrubbed too hard. Both the ears fell off.

I said, "Grandpa! I'm not sure this is the right way to fix my bear."

"Never you mind now," Grandpa said. "He'll be as good as new in no time."

Grandpa rinsed my bear and squeezed him hard. Then he shook him out.

I told him, "Grandpa, a clean bear's not so good if it's all flat and wrinkled and hasn't any ears!"

"Never you mind now," Grandpa said.

Then he hung my bear outside to dry, with one ear on each side.

He said, "I have to go downtown to buy new stuffing. Anybody want to come along?"

I did.

By the time we got back home again, my bear and his ears were dry. He was still all flat and broken.

I said, "Grandpa? Are you sure . . ."

I guess you know what Grandpa said. We sat down outside again. Grandpa filled my bear with new fluffy stuffing.

He put about a hundred hunks of stuffing in the arms. He put about a hundred hunks of stuffing in the legs. Then he put about a hundred hunks of stuffing in the head and in the nose and in the neck.

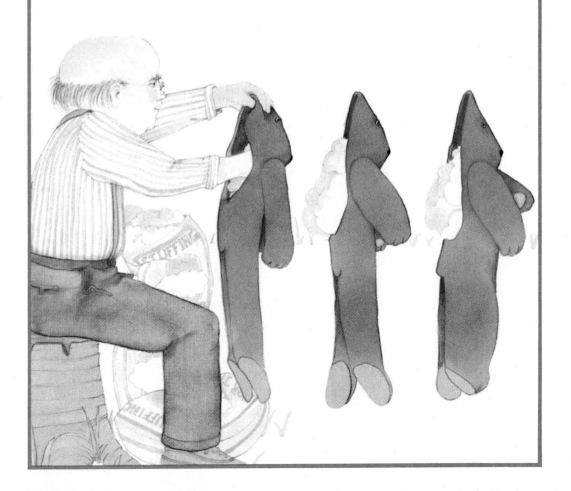

The stomach still looked hungry. So Grandpa kept on stuffing.

Then I brought him a needle and thread. Grandpa sewed the back of my bear and said, "There . . ."

"Wait a minute, Grandpa!" I said. "He isn't dirty anymore. He isn't flat or wrinkled. But he still doesn't look so good without . . ."

200

"Never you mind," Grandpa said. "I can fix that too."

Then Grandpa sewed on the ears.

I turned my bear all around and carefully looked it over.

"Grandpa," I said at last. "I thought you could fix anything. But this bear isn't as good as new."

There was a long silence. Grandpa looked kind of sad.

"It's **better** than new!" I shouted, laughing.

I gave Grandpa my best bear hug.

Now whenever K.C. comes to visit, Grandpa and I grab our hats and my bear. Then we slip out the back door, neverminding.

What Are You Wearing?

boots

These **boots** are too big.

coat

In winter, you need a warm **coat.**

hats

Do you like my **hats?**

mittens

Kate's **mittens** are red.

ribbon

Mary has a **ribbon**
in her hair.

shirt

Bob's old **shirt** is
too small now.

sunglasses

Oliver has new
sunglasses.

Family

baby

Shh! The **baby** is sleeping.

grandma

Grandma takes Luke for a walk.

mother

Mother takes care of me if I get hurt.

son

Kevin is Mr. Brown's **son.**

Us

hair

Hattie has long **hair.**

hands

Wash your **hands** before you eat.

knees

Mark's **knees** are cold.

tooth

Lizzy's **tooth** came out today.

Places

beach

I have fun at the **beach.**

cage

The tiger is in a **cage.**

den

A bear lives in a **den.**

hospital

When Jake got sick,
he went to the **hospital.**

house

The **house** has a tree in front.

neighborhood

Does your **neighborhood** look like this?

town

This small **town** has one school.

woods

Different kinds of trees grow in the **woods.**

Animals

alligator

Stay away from
the **alligator!**

cat

Ed likes to pat his **cat.**

dog

My **dog** runs with me.

fox

The **fox** ran into
the woods.

frog

The **frog** will soon
catch that bug.

mouse

The little **mouse** hid
between the logs.

snake

A **snake** was under
the rock.

squirrel

The **squirrel** is
in a tree.

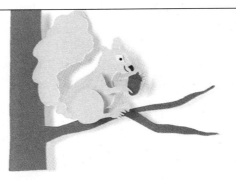

People

children

The **children** are playing.

friends

Kim and I are
best **friends**.

neighbor

Miss Willet is our
neighbor.

teacher

The **teacher** reads
to the children.

Colors

brown

The bear has **brown** fur.

pink

Elena blows up a
pink balloon.

white

White clouds move
across the sky.

rainbow

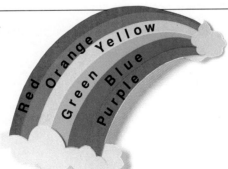

Things We Do

buy

I will **buy** a hat today.

carry

Max can **carry**
a big bag.

catch

Amanda can **catch** a ball.

climbs

Our cat **climbs** trees.

dance

I like to see Mother
and Daddy **dance.**

hug

Grandpa gives me a **hug.**

kiss

I **kiss** my baby sister.

whispered

Kate **whispered**
in Mary's ear.

At Home

bath

Drew takes a **bath.**

blanket

The **blanket** keeps Carlos warm at night.

chair

We all like this **chair** best.

closet

My hat is in the **closet.**

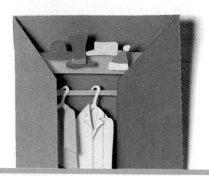

ladder

You can use a **ladder**
to go up high.

radio

I like to hear the **radio**.

rug

Spot sleeps
on the red **rug**.

table

The food is on the **table**.

Food and Eating

bite

Take a **bite** of
the apple.

bread

Clara cut
the warm **bread.**

breakfast

We eat **breakfast**
in the morning.

cook

Joe can **cook** fish
in a pan.

Having Fun

climb

Meg likes to **climb**
a tree.

fishing

Luke is going **fishing**.

puppet

Did you see the
puppet show?

skateboard

Kevin zooms along
on his **skateboard**.

On the Farm

ducks

The **ducks** swim
in a line.

fence

Rob sits on the **fence.**

grows

The corn **grows** very tall.

pail

Use the **pail** to carry
water.

pigs

Grandma gives food to the **pigs.**

pond

Cows drink from the **pond.**

rake

Rob can **rake** the hay.

tree

Jenny is up in a big **tree.**

Sizes

fat

The **fat** toad sits on a rock.

huge

What **huge** ears!

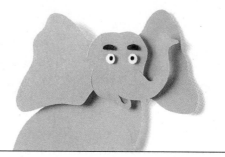

long

That is a **long** neck.

small

Ants are very **small** bugs.

In a Garden

butterfly

A **butterfly** is sitting on a leaf.

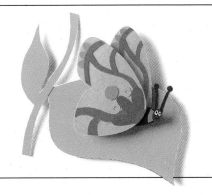

flowers

Mrs. Lee picked the yellow **flowers.**

plants

We have many **plants** in our garden.

seeds

The bean plants grew from little **seeds.**